Ten Red Sleds

by Padraig George
illustrated by Jaime Smith

Phonics Skill: Short *Ee* /e/
High-Frequency Words: *here, go, from*

PEARSON

Scott
Foresman

Look, Nan! Look, Nat!
Dad, get the red sleds.

Get Ben! Get Sam!

Ben and Sam have red sleds.

Ben, tell Ken to get a sled.

Ken, get a red sled.

Bill, get Don and Dan.

Don and Dan, get a sled from Bill.

Dad, get a sled for little Ted.
We have sleds. Here we go!

Look at ten red sleds go!

Ten red sleds go from end to end.

We get to the end.
Ten red sleds, here we go.